I0019983

Tech Horizons 2024

Navigating the New Frontier of Technology

David Wilson

Tech Horizons 2024

All rights reserved. No part of this publication may be reproduced, distributed, or transmitted in any form or by any means, including photocopying, recording, or other electronic or mechanical methods, without the prior written permission of the publisher, except in the case of brief quotations embodied in critical reviews and certain other noncommercial uses permitted by copyright law.

© David Wilson, 2024.

Table of Contents

Tech Horizons 2024

Introduction

The only thing that is consistent in the rapidly changing world of technology is change. We see the quick development of technology with every year that goes by, resulting in new breakthroughs, fads, and opportunities. Technological developments in a number of areas, including robots, data science, artificial intelligence, and more, are quickening the rate of change. We will explore the importance of accepting the swift advancement of technology and comprehending the influence of new trends in this introduction.

Welcoming the Quick Advancement of Technology

Technology is developing at a rapid pace, which offers opportunities and challenges to organisations, individuals, and society at large. Accepting this evolution means adjusting to the constant changes in technology and using them to spur innovation, boost productivity, and meet societal demands.

A fundamental element of accepting technological advancement is the mental adjustment needed to welcome change. Modern technology is developing at a rapid pace, making conventional ways of doing things outdated very quickly in the digital age. In order to embrace this rapid transformation, people and organisations must develop a growth mindset, which is typified by resilience, adaptability, and a desire to grow.

Adopting technological evolution also means keeping abreast of the most recent advancements, trends, and breakthroughs in the realm of technology. This entails actively searching for information via a variety of sources, including trade journals, webinars, conferences, and internet discussion boards. People who keep up with the latest developments in technology can spot new possibilities, predict rising trends, and set themselves up for success in a constantly shifting field.

Accepting technological advancement also necessitates a willingness to try new things and take chances. Innovation frequently arises from trial and error and experimenting in a setting that is changing quickly. Driving significant change and achieving ground-breaking outcomes is more likely for people and organisations that are ready to experiment with new technology and methods and take measured risks.

Finally, cultivating a culture of cooperation and information exchange is a crucial part of accepting technological advancement. In the globally connected world of today, settings that encourage the free interchange of ideas and the importance of many points of view are frequently more conducive to creativity.

Organisations may leverage the collective intelligence of their teams to drive innovation and problem-solving at scale by cultivating a collaborative culture.

Understanding the Impact of Emerging Trends

Emerging technological trends have an impact on almost every part of our lives, from how we work and communicate to how we get information and pass the time, going well beyond the world of technology itself. In order to properly traverse the intricacies of the modern technology world, individuals and organisations must have a thorough understanding of the effects of these developments.

Emerging technology developments have a profound impact on many industries and sectors, which is one of their main effects. Artificial intelligence, blockchain, and the Internet of Things (IoT) are a few examples of the technologies that are upending established business structures, opening up new avenues for value generation, and achieving previously unheard-of levels of productivity and efficiency.

Furthermore, the nature of employment and the competencies needed to succeed in the digital economy are changing as a result of new technological advances. Programming, digital literacy, and data analysis are among the talents that are in high demand as automation, AI, and robotics continue to progress. Those who have these abilities will be in a better position to prosper in a labour market that is becoming more and more competitive and to make a significant contribution to their organisations' digital transformation.

Moreover, new developments in technology are bringing about societal transformation, impacting not only healthcare and education but also governance and entertainment.

Technologies like telemedicine, augmented reality, and virtual reality are completely changing how we communicate, acquire new skills, and receive healthcare. In a similar vein, developments in digital money, smart cities, and renewable energy are influencing urbanisation, sustainability, and financial inclusion in the future.

To sum up, in order for people and organisations to succeed in the digital era, they must embrace the rapid growth of technology and recognise the implications of new trends. In a technical environment that is always evolving, people can position themselves for success by adopting a growth mindset, remaining informed, and being open to experimenting. Likewise, organisations may spur innovation, add value, and support constructive social change by realising the transformative power of emerging trends and seizing their opportunities.

Chapter 1: Generative-AI

The field of artificial intelligence (AI) has advanced significantly in recent years, with generative AI emerging as one of the most revolutionary innovations. With the potential to produce content that closely mimics human-generated work, this ground-breaking technology has the potential to transform a number of sectors and provide entirely new avenues for creativity and innovation. This chapter will examine the ways in which generative AI is changing the way that content is created, as well as how it may be applied to data science and AI research and how it will influence the creative industries going forward.

Transforming the Production of Contents

Generative AI, sometimes referred to as AI creativity or creative AI, is the process of using artificial intelligence algorithms to produce material on their own. This material is generated using patterns and data fed into the AI model during training, and it can be text, photos, music, videos, and more. Generative AI can produce large amounts of content fast and effectively, in contrast to traditional content production techniques, which depend on human input and creativity.

The capacity of generative AI to generate varied and high-quality material is one of its main features. Generative AI algorithms may learn to imitate the style, tone, and organization of human-generated content by examining vast amounts of existing content.

This allows them to produce output that is virtually identical to the original. This creates new opportunities for content production in a variety of sectors, including marketing, advertising, and journalism in addition to entertainment.

Additionally, content producers can automate tedious processes and optimize their workflow with the help of generative AI. Creators can concentrate their time and efforts on more strategic and creative areas of their work, such brainstorming, storytelling, and audience interaction, by using AI algorithms to generate content. In addition to boosting output, this also gives artists the freedom to experiment with various forms and styles as well as new creative directions.

Additionally, by making content production more accessible to people and organizations with less means or experience, generative AI has the potential to democratize the process of creating content. Anybody, regardless of background or skill level, may use Generative AI to produce professional-quality content thanks to the development of user-friendly AI tools and platforms. This may unleash a new generation of artists and storytellers and democratize access to creative expression.

Data Science and AI Research Applications

Apart from its uses in content production, generative AI is propelling important developments in data science and AI research. Generative AI algorithms are being used by researchers and data scientists to create artificial intelligence (AI) data, model intricate situations, and investigate new approaches to solving practical issues.

The creation of sophisticated generative models is one of the main uses of generative AI in AI research. Based on the patterns and features discovered from training data, these models—Generative Adversarial Networks, or GANs, and Variational Autoencoders, or VAEs—can create realistic pictures, movies, and audio samples from start. This has broad ramifications for domains where producing realistic and varied data is crucial for training and assessment, like computer vision, natural language processing, and speech synthesis.

Generative AI is being utilized to enhance conventional data analysis methodologies and approaches in addition to generative models. Data scientists can get around issues like skewed datasets, data shortages, and privacy problems by creating synthetic data that closely mimics real-world data. As a result, they are able to train machine learning models that are more reliable and broadly applicable, which improves predictions, insights, and decision-making.

In the area of creative computing, where academics are looking for novel ways to incorporate AI algorithms into the creative process, generative AI is also spurring innovation.

Researchers are creating artificial intelligence (AI) systems that can work with human creators to generate ideas, co-create material autonomously, and cooperate using generative models in conjunction with approaches like reinforcement learning and interactive design. By pushing the frontiers of innovation, this interdisciplinary approach is opening up new avenues for human-machine collaboration.

Creative Industries: Shaping Their Future

Advertising, entertainment, design, and other creative industries are going to see radical changes in the future because to generative AI. Generative AI is redefining the creation, consumption, and commercialization of content by automating monotonous processes, producing tailored content, and opening up new avenues for innovation.

For instance, generative AI is being utilized in the advertising sector to develop customized marketing campaigns, target audience segments with content, and instantly improve ad performance. AI algorithms may provide personalized advertising that connect with customers by evaluating user data and preferences. This results in more consumer engagement, higher conversion rates, and a better return on investment for marketers.

Similar to this, generative AI is opening up new storytelling, interactive, and immersive media opportunities in the entertainment sector.

AI algorithms are changing how audiences interact with and consume entertainment content. Examples include dynamic storylines, personalized content recommendations, and virtual reality and augmented reality experiences. This could completely transform the entertainment sector, opening up new doors for distributors, consumers, and content producers.

Furthermore, generative AI is enabling designers to push the frontiers of artistic expression, automate laborious activities, and investigate new creative possibilities in the design business.

AI algorithms can help designers with the creative process, resulting in more impactful and inventive designs, by producing design variations, investigating alternative concepts, and forecasting consumer preferences. This could revolutionize the way goods are created, used, and perceived, spurring creativity and distinction in cutthroat markets.

In summary, generative AI is reshaping the creative industries, propelling breakthroughs in data science and AI research, and transforming content production. Researchers, data scientists, and content creators are pushing the frontiers of creativity, innovation, and human-machine collaboration by utilizing the ability of AI algorithms to develop content autonomously. With its further development and maturation, generative AI has the potential to revolutionize content creation, consumption, and interaction in the digital age, opening up new avenues of possibility.

Chapter 2: Computing Power

Computing power is a key component of the rapidly changing technological landscape, propelling innovation and influencing how we interact with the digital world. This chapter discusses the history of computing infrastructure, the potential it brings in robotics and data analytics, and how to manage the impending 6G era.

The Evolution of Computing Infrastructure

The history of computing infrastructure begins with the invention of mechanical calculators and punch cards and continues through the development of integrated circuits, transistors, and vacuum tubes. Computing power has increased significantly with each development, allowing for greater processing speeds, more storage space, and more effective data management.

These days, computing infrastructure includes a huge network of linked devices, ranging from cloud servers and data centers to laptops and cellphones. Because of this integrated environment, people, businesses, and organizations may use computer power for a wide range of jobs and applications with ease. It also facilitates seamless communication, collaboration, and processing.

Moore's Law—which states that a microchip's transistor count doubles roughly every two years, increasing computing power—is one of the main forces behind the expansion of computing infrastructure.

This rapid expansion has spurred breakthroughs in fields like big data analytics, machine learning, and artificial intelligence, opening up new avenues for technical development.

Furthermore, the introduction of cloud computing has completely changed how computer resources are allocated, controlled, and accessed. Cloud services enable businesses to quickly develop applications, extend infrastructure, and adjust to changing demands by providing scalable and on-demand access to computing power, storage, and networking resources.

Data Science and Robotics Opportunities

Revolutionary developments in robotics and data science have been made possible by the expansion of computing power availability. Combining computer science, statistics, and domain knowledge, data science is a multidisciplinary field that uses computing power to analyze large volumes of data, extract insights, and make data-driven decisions.

Computing power makes it possible to train and implement sophisticated machine learning models, like deep neural networks and reinforcement learning algorithms, in the field of data science.

These models have the potential to revolutionize fields like healthcare, banking, and autonomous systems because of their extraordinary accuracy in processing large datasets, spotting patterns, and making predictions.

In a similar vein, processing capacity is necessary for the control and coordination of robotic systems in robotics, an interdisciplinary topic spanning computer science and engineering. Robots can now sense their surroundings, plan and carry out activities, and communicate with humans and other machines in real time thanks to high-performance computing, which creates opportunities in industries like manufacturing, logistics, and healthcare.

Moreover, robotics and data science coming together is spurring innovation in domains including motion planning, robotic perception, and human-robot interaction.

Researchers and engineers are creating intelligent robotic systems that can navigate, manipulate, and make decisions on their own. These systems have the potential to revolutionize industries and change society by combining sophisticated sensors, algorithms, and actuators.

Navigating the Era of 6G

The future of digital infrastructure and connectivity will be greatly influenced by computational power as we go into the era of 6G, the next generation of wireless communication. Unprecedented speed, capacity, and dependability are promised by 6G, opening the door for ground-breaking applications like telemedicine, autonomous cars, and augmented reality.

With 6G, edge computing, distributed processing, and network intelligence will all be included in the computing capability that goes beyond conventional data centers and cloud servers. This distributed computing paradigm will make it possible to run high-bandwidth, low-latency applications like immersive gaming, smart cities, and remote surgery that call for real-time processing and reaction.

Furthermore, 6G will spur developments in quantum computing, AI, and machine learning, opening up new possibilities and avenues for creativity. Autonomous systems, predictive analytics, and tailored services will be made possible by AI-powered networks, intelligent edge devices, and quantum-enhanced algorithms, which will revolutionize industries and change society.

To sum up, computational power is fostering innovation and facilitating game-changing developments in wireless communication, robotics, and data science.

The computing infrastructure will keep changing as we move through the 6G era, offering new opportunities and difficulties for people, companies, and society at large. We may open up new possibilities and influence the direction of technology in a world that is changing quickly by utilizing computational power.

Chapter 3: Smart(er) Devices

The proliferation of smart gadgets has become pervasive in an era of rapid technological innovation, altering our interactions with technology and boosting productivity across a range of sectors. This chapter examines how AI-powered gadgets can improve productivity, the need for automation engineers and IT managers, and how smarter technologies are revolutionizing the workplace.

Improving Productivity with AI-Powered Devices

A new era of efficiency and convenience has been ushered in by the incorporation of artificial intelligence (AI) into smart gadgets. Artificial intelligence (AI)-enabled gadgets utilize machine learning algorithms to automate activities, analyze data, and forecast user behavior. This leads to more efficient workflows and higher productivity.

Artificial intelligence (AI)-enabled virtual assistants, like Apple's Siri and Amazon's Alexa, can handle a variety of duties, including answering questions, controlling smart home devices, and setting reminders and calendars. By using machine learning and natural language processing, these virtual assistants can comprehend and react to human orders, offering individualized support and lessening the cognitive burden on users.

Similar to this, AI-powered smart home appliances like lighting controls, security cameras, and thermostats can optimize energy use, boost security, and raise comfort levels in response to user preferences and behavior. These gadgets use sensors, data analytics, and predictive modeling to automate repetitive operations and adjust to shifting environmental circumstances. This reduces energy consumption and improves user ease.

Additionally, people may track their health and wellness in real-time with AI-driven devices like fitness trackers and health monitors, which offer insights into physiological parameters, activity levels, and sleep patterns. With the help of these gadgets, people can make better lifestyle and behavioral choices, which will enhance their general well-being and health.

Demand for Automation Engineers and IT Managers

The demand for IT managers and automation engineers who can develop, implement, and oversee complex systems and networks is rising as a result of the widespread use of smart devices. When it comes to ensuring that smart technologies are compatible, secure, and scalable across a variety of platforms and devices, IT managers are essential to the process.

Conversely, automation engineers focus on creating and implementing automation solutions that use robotic process automation (RPA), artificial intelligence (AI), and machine learning to streamline workflows and business processes. These experts create and deploy software robots that swiftly and accurately complete repetitive jobs like data input, document processing, and customer support, freeing up human resources for more planned and innovative projects.

Additionally, integrating AI-driven devices into business environments calls for a high level of proficiency in data privacy, cybersecurity, and regulatory compliance. To reduce the risks of illegal access, data breaches, and cyberattacks, IT managers and automation engineers must make sure that smart devices follow industry standards and best practices for data protection and security.

Improving Workplace Experience with Intelligent Technologies

Smarter technology adoption is changing the workplace by facilitating flexible scheduling, remote collaboration, and customized experiences. Regardless of location or time zone, employees can work more productively, communicate more effectively, and collaborate more easily with the help of AI-driven gadgets and automation solutions.

For instance, real-time meeting transcription, key point summaries, and action item generation are all possible with AI-powered virtual meeting assistants like Zoom's transcription function and Microsoft's Cortana integration.

These features improve accessibility and efficiency for participants who are unable to attend in person. These assistants enable more effective communication and decision-making by interpreting speech and extracting pertinent information using machine learning and natural language processing.

Additionally, employees may automate tedious operations and streamline corporate processes with AI-driven workflow automation platforms like Microsoft Power Automate and Zapier, all without the need for advanced programming expertise or technical abilities.

By providing a library of pre-built connectors and workflows that can be modified and adapted to particular use cases, these platforms help businesses maximize productivity and minimize human labor.

In conclusion, AI-powered smart gadgets are transforming the workplace by improving productivity, efficiency, and teamwork in a variety of fields. As more businesses look to use technology to spur innovation and gain a competitive edge, there is a growing need for IT managers and automation engineers. Businesses may revolutionize the workplace, empower staff members, and open up new avenues for development and success in the digital era by adopting smarter technologies.

Chapter 4: Datafication

Data is now essential to modern civilization in an increasingly digital age, since it fosters economic growth, innovation, and decision-making. This chapter examines the emergence of data-driven technologies, data science and engineering vocations, and the potential and problems associated with data analysis and security in the digital age.

Data-driven Technology's Ascent

"Datafication" describes the process of converting different facets of human existence and behavior into digital information. Almost every facet of contemporary life creates copious amounts of data that may be gathered, saved, and analyzed, from sensor readings and GPS locations to online transactions and social media interactions.

Data-driven technology has become increasingly popular as a result of advancements in computing power, storage capacity, and data processing algorithms.

These developments have made it possible for enterprises to glean actionable intelligence and valuable insights from vast and varied datasets. Data-driven technologies are turning industries upside down and changing how people work, live, and engage with the world. Examples of these include social media networks, e-commerce platforms, healthcare systems, and smart cities.

In the retail sector, for instance, datafication helps companies to evaluate consumer behavior, preferences, and purchase trends in order to improve customer experience, optimize inventory management, and customize marketing efforts.

Similar to this, data-driven technologies are used in healthcare to improve patient care, detect illnesses, and create individualized treatment regimens. These technologies include wearable sensors, medical imaging data, and electronic health records.

Data Science and Engineering Careers

The increasing need for qualified individuals with expertise in data science and engineering who can leverage data to spur innovation and resolve challenging issues is a result of the emergence of "datafication." In order to extract insights and guide decision-making, data scientists, data engineers, and data analysts play crucial roles in the collection, processing, and analysis of data.

In order to find patterns, trends, and correlations in data, data scientists specialize in creating prediction models, machine learning algorithms, and statistical methodologies. They can recognize opportunities for data-driven innovation and optimization because they have a solid background in computer science, statistics, mathematics, and domain-specific knowledge.

Large-scale data processing, analysis, and storage can be accomplished more effectively by using scalable data infrastructure and systems, which is the specialty of data engineers.

They can design and implement reliable data pipelines and analytics platforms because they are skilled in distributed computing, cloud computing, and database administration.

By converting technical insights into practical recommendations and strategic insights, data analysts help to close the gap between data science and business. Their robust analytical ability, business acumen, and communication skills allow them to effectively assess data, produce reports, and share results with stakeholders.

Securing and Analyzing Data in the Digital Age

Organizations are having an increasing amount of difficulty safeguarding and interpreting data in the digital age as datafication keeps growing. Businesses face serious risks and liabilities from data security breaches, privacy issues, and regulatory compliance requirements. As a result, strong data governance, encryption, and access control procedures are required.

Data management, storage, and analysis are further complicated by the sheer amount, velocity, and variety of data produced by data-driven technology. Scalable infrastructure, data integration, and analytics tools are necessary investments for organizations to handle and extract knowledge from big and varied datasets.

In order for businesses to maximize operations, enhance decision-making, and spur innovation, data analytics is essential to obtaining actionable knowledge from data. Businesses can use data-driven insights to identify trends, reduce risks, and seize opportunities in real-time. These insights can be found in descriptive, diagnostic, predictive, or prescriptive analytics.

In conclusion, datafication is changing how we live, work, and engage with the world around us. It is also changing industries. As businesses want to use data-driven technology to spur innovation and gain a competitive edge, jobs in data science and engineering are in great demand. Through efficient data security and analysis, companies may fully realize the benefits of datafication and leverage data to drive expansion and prosperity in the digital era.

Chapter 5: Machine Learning and Artificial Intelligence (AI)

The fields of artificial intelligence (AI) and machine learning (ML) have seen significant changes as a result of these game-changing technologies. This chapter examines their effects on various industries, employment prospects in data analysis and AI development, and their influence on how automation and decision-making will develop in the future.

Impact on Various Sectors

AI and ML technologies are transforming a wide range of industries, including manufacturing, retail, healthcare, and finance. AI-powered diagnostic technologies are revolutionizing the healthcare industry by analyzing medical images, identifying illnesses, and helping medical professionals make precise diagnosis and treatment choices.

Similar to this, AI algorithms are utilized in finance for algorithmic trading, risk assessment, and fraud detection. These applications help financial institutions increase efficiency and security while optimizing profits.

Artificial intelligence (AI)-driven robotics and automation technologies are simplifying production procedures, raising efficiency, and cutting expenses in the manufacturing sector. Real-time sensor data analysis by ML algorithms can be used to forecast maintenance requirements, maximize equipment performance, and minimize expensive downtime.

By providing customized product recommendations based on past purchase behavior and preferences, AI-powered recommendation systems in retail enhance customer satisfaction, boost sales, and personalize customer experiences.

Career Opportunities in Data Analysis and AI Development

The need for qualified experts in data analysis and AI development is rising as a result of the swift development of ML and AI technologies. Jobs like data scientist, data analyst, AI engineer, and machine learning engineer are highly sought after in a variety of industries.

AI engineers are experts at creating and applying deep learning models, neural networks, and AI algorithms to tackle challenging issues and spur innovation. Their proficiency in programming languages, including Python, TensorFlow, and PyTorch, allows them to create and implement scalable artificial intelligence solutions.

To achieve optimal performance, machine learning engineers concentrate on developing and training machine learning models, adjusting hyperparameters, and optimizing algorithms. Because of their solid foundation in computer science, statistics, and mathematics, they are able to create algorithms and predictive models that draw conclusions from data.

To extract actionable insights from large and complex datasets, data scientists use techniques such as statistical analysis, machine learning, and data visualization. Their strong domain knowledge, programming skills, and analytical aptitude allow them to find patterns, trends, and correlations in data that drive innovation and help make business decisions.

Data analysts are experts at gathering, preparing, and interpreting data to produce dashboards, reports, and visualizations that help explain insights and facilitate decision-making. They can convert data into actionable intelligence that propels business success because they have strong quantitative, data manipulation, and communication skills.

Shaping the Future of Automation and Decision Making

Organizations can now automate repetitive tasks, optimize processes, and make data-driven decisions instantly thanks to AI and ML technologies, which are reshaping automation and decision-making in the future.

AI and ML are accelerating innovation and changing industries with applications ranging from virtual assistants and driverless cars to predictive maintenance and supply chain optimization.

Without human assistance, autonomous cars perceive their surroundings, negotiate obstacles, and make driving decisions using AI algorithms and sensor data. Natural language processing and machine learning techniques are used by virtual assistants like

Siri, Alexa, and Google Assistant to comprehend user queries, retrieve information, and carry out tasks on their behalf.

Predictive maintenance systems allow organizations to schedule maintenance proactively and identify potential failures before they happen by using machine learning (ML) algorithms to analyze sensor data and identify anomalies in equipment performance.

Artificial intelligence (AI) algorithms are used by supply chain optimization systems to assess demand forecasts, optimize inventory levels, and reduce costs while maximizing efficiency.

In summary, AI and ML technologies are transforming a number of industries and spurring innovation in others. There are many job opportunities in data analysis and AI development, and there is a great need for qualified individuals who can use ML and AI to solve challenging problems and propel business success. AI and ML are laying the foundation for a more productive, intelligent, and efficient future by influencing automation and decision-making in the future.

Chapter 6: Extended Reality

With the ability to create immersive experiences that combine the real and digital worlds, Extended Reality (XR) includes virtual reality (VR), augmented reality (AR), and mixed reality (MR). This chapter explores the uses of virtual reality (XR) in marketing, gaming, and training, as well as the variety of job options in this emerging industry.

Immersive Experiences with VR, AR, and Mixed Reality

A number of facets of our life are improved by the realistic and engaging interactions that consumers may have with digital information thanks to VR, AR, and MR technology. While MR perfectly combines virtual and physical elements, AR overlays digital information over the actual world, and VR immerses people in fully digital surroundings.

VR gaming gives users the chance to dive into completely immersive virtual environments where they can explore exotic settings, go on exhilarating adventures, and communicate in real time with virtual characters and things. AR games, on the other hand, combine digital components with the real world of the user to create dynamic, interactive gaming environments in common places. VR and AR components are combined in MR games to let users interact with virtual items superimposed on the actual environment.

XR technologies offer interactive experiences and realistic simulations that improve learning outcomes and skill development in training and education. VR training simulations, which include industrial training scenarios, flying simulators, and medical procedures, allow users to practice difficult skills in a safe and controlled environment. AR educational apps increase learning for students of all ages by superimposing instructional content onto real-world objects.

XR technologies provide marketers and advertisers with creative approaches to enthrall and engage consumers, resulting in immersive and memorable brand experiences.

By enabling users to connect with virtual goods and experiences in their own settings, augmented reality marketing campaigns increase brand engagement and purchase intent. Users are taken to virtual showrooms, events, and places through VR marketing experiences, creating memorable and engaging brand encounters.

Training, Marketing, and Gaming Applications

With the help of VR, AR, and MR, the gaming industry has quickly embraced XR technologies, pushing the limits of interactive entertainment and producing captivating, immersive gaming experiences. XR technologies are revolutionizing how we play and interact with games, from VR headsets and controllers to AR-capable smartphone apps and mixed reality gaming experiences.

With immersive simulations and interactive experiences that improve learning outcomes and skill development, XR technologies are transforming traditional learning approaches in training and education. With the help of virtual reality training simulations, users can rehearse difficult tasks in lifelike settings, including medical procedures, emergency response training, and vocational skill development. AR educational apps increase learning for students of all ages by superimposing instructional content onto real-world objects.

XR technologies in marketing and advertising are opening up new avenues for brands to interact and establish creative connections with customers.

By bridging the gap between the real and digital worlds, marketers can build interactive experiences using augmented reality marketing campaigns that let customers interact with virtual goods and experiences in the comfort of their own homes. Users are taken to virtual showrooms, events, and places through VR marketing experiences, creating memorable and engaging brand encounters.

Exploring Extended Reality Career Paths

The need for qualified individuals in a variety of professions across the sector has arisen from the XR technologies' increasing popularity. The field of extended reality offers a variety of professional possibilities, from content makers and developers to designers and engineers.

The creation of interactive content and immersive experiences for VR, AR, and MR platforms is largely dependent on content creators. In order to create engaging and captivating user experiences, they might specialize in 3D modeling, animation, sound design, or narrative storytelling.

Programming languages like C#, C++, and Unity are used by developers to create interactive environments, games, and simulations. Developers are in charge of designing the software and apps that drive XR experiences. Depending on their hobbies and skill set, they might focus on developing VR apps, AR apps, or MR content.

Designers concentrate on user interface (UI) and user experience (UX), producing user-friendly and immersive interfaces that improve the user's experience in MR, VR, and AR environments. They might work in tandem with developers and content producers to create interactive interfaces, navigational aids, and eye-catching visuals that maximize user experience and engagement.

The technologies that power XR experiences, such VR headsets, AR glasses, and MR devices, are designed and optimized by engineers who specialize in hardware and software development. Depending on their specialty, they could work on software optimization, firmware development, or hardware design.

In summary, immersive experiences that combine the actual and virtual worlds are made possible by extended reality (XR) technologies, which are revolutionizing marketing, training, and gaming. Extended reality offers workers a plethora of employment options in content creation, development, design, and engineering, all of which can lead to fulfilling careers in the industry.

Chapter 7: Digital Trust

Digital trust, which includes people's and organizations' trust and dependability in digital technologies, is the cornerstone of our contemporary digital economy. This chapter looks at the value of developing confidence in digital technology, the ethical hacking and cybersecurity fields, and the methods for protecting digital assets and privacy in a world where communication is becoming more and more interconnected.

Developing Confidence in Digital Technologies

In this day of digitalization, trust is necessary to promote creativity, propel economic expansion, and guarantee the seamless operation of our globalized society. The confidence that people and organizations have in the security, dependability, and integrity of digital technologies, platforms, and services is referred to as digital trust.

Establishing digital trust necessitates a multidimensional strategy that touches on several facets of data privacy, cybersecurity, and moral technology use. In order to do this, strong security measures must be put in place, data protection laws must be followed, and digital technology use must be transparent and accountable.

By investing in cybersecurity policies and technology, putting robust authentication and encryption mechanisms in place, and routinely auditing and monitoring their systems for threats and vulnerabilities, organizations may increase digital trust.

Additionally, they may show their dedication to data privacy and transparency by establishing privacy policies that are simple to understand and follow, getting user consent for data collection and processing, and responding quickly to any security incidents or breaches.

Using strong and distinctive passwords, updating software and hardware with security patches, and exercising caution when disclosing personal information online are all examples of good cyber hygiene that people can do to support digital trust. Through proactive measures to safeguard their digital identities and privacy, individuals can contribute to the establishment of a digital culture that is characterized by trust and security.

Ethical hacking and cybersecurity careers

The need for qualified cybersecurity and ethical hacking specialists has increased due to the growing significance of digital trust. These experts are essential for preserving digital assets, preserving data privacy, and thwarting online threats and attacks.

The design, implementation, and management of security solutions that shield an organization's digital assets and infrastructure from online threats and attacks fall within the purview of cybersecurity specialists. Depending on their abilities and interests, they might focus on information security management, endpoint security, cloud security, network security, or information security management.

Cybersecurity professionals that specialize in finding and taking advantage of weaknesses in systems and networks to evaluate their security posture are called ethical hackers, sometimes referred to as penetration testers or white-hat hackers. They assist companies in identifying and fixing security flaws before bad actors can take advantage of them by using their expertise to undertake authorized security assessments, penetration testing, and vulnerability assessments.

A vital role in safeguarding enterprises from cyber threats and guaranteeing the availability and integrity of their digital assets is played by security analysts, incident responders, forensic analysts, and security architects, among other occupations in cybersecurity and ethical hacking.

Protecting Privacy and Digital Assets

Protecting digital assets and privacy is critical in today's globalized world, since cyberattacks and data breaches put people, businesses, and society at large at serious danger. Organizations and people alike must take a proactive and all-encompassing approach to cybersecurity and data protection in order to safeguard digital assets and privacy.

Employing strong security measures, such encryption, access controls, and intrusion detection systems, can help organizations secure digital assets and privacy by preventing unauthorized access to and disclosure of sensitive data. To teach staff members about cybersecurity best practices and the value of data privacy, they can also fund employee training and awareness initiatives.

By being cautious while sharing personal information online, utilizing strong and distinctive passwords, activating multi-factor authentication, and being watchful over the security of their devices and accounts, people can safeguard their digital assets and privacy.

Additionally, they can safeguard their online transactions and conversations by utilizing privacy-enhancing technologies like encrypted messaging apps and virtual private networks (VPNs).

To sum up, the development of digital trust is critical to innovation, economic expansion, and the seamless operation of our globalized society. Individuals and organizations may help create a better and more secure digital environment for everyone by increasing their confidence in digital technology, pursuing professions in cybersecurity and ethical hacking, and protecting digital assets and privacy.

Chapter 8: 3D Printing

Prototyping and Manufacturing Innovations

Additive manufacturing, commonly referred to as 3D printing, has completely changed manufacturing and prototyping procedures in a variety of sectors. In contrast to conventional subtractive manufacturing techniques that entail removing material from a solid block, 3D printing constructs objects layer by layer, providing more efficiency, customization, and design freedom.

Rapid prototyping, which enables engineers and designers to swiftly produce tangible prototypes of their designs for testing and validation, is one of the major advancements made possible by 3D printing. Faster product development cycles, shorter time to market, and lower costs compared to traditional prototype methods are all made possible by this iterative process.

Apart from prototype, 3D printing has revolutionized manufacturing procedures by permitting mass customisation, personalization, and on-demand production. Businesses may now create intricately geometrized, sophisticated parts and components that would be difficult or impossible to fabricate with conventional methods. Because of its adaptability and versatility, 3D printing has become widely used in a variety of industries, including consumer goods, automotive, aerospace, and healthcare.

Prospects for 3D printing, AI, and machine learning

There are many of intriguing prospects for innovation and expansion where machine learning, 3D printing, and artificial intelligence (AI) converge. Improved performance, efficiency, and reliability can be achieved by using AI and machine learning algorithms to optimize the design, simulation, and optimization of 3D printed parts and components.

AI-driven generative design algorithms, for instance, can produce optimum designs automatically based on predetermined performance standards, such heat conductivity, structural integrity, or weight reduction.

Large design spaces can be explored by these algorithms, which can then find ideal solutions that human designers could not have thought of, producing lighter, stronger, and more effective parts.

In order to identify and anticipate problems, optimize printing parameters, and enhance print quality and dependability, machine learning algorithms can also evaluate data from 3D printing operations. Manufacturers may improve process control, save waste, and boost efficiency in 3D printing operations by utilizing machine learning approaches.

Additive Manufacturing Transforming Industries

By facilitating new business models, product innovations, and supply chain efficiencies, additive manufacturing has the potential to completely change a number of sectors. For instance, businesses in the aerospace sector are employing 3D printing to create intricate, lightweight parts and components for spacecraft and airplanes, which lowers fuel consumption and boosts efficiency.

By making it possible to produce personalized implants, prosthetics, and medical equipment that are suited to each patient's unique anatomy, 3D printing is completely changing the way that healthcare is provided to patients.

With the assistance of 3D printed models, surgeons can now plan and perform intricate surgeries, improving results and lowering surgical risks.

3D printing is being used by automakers to create lightweight, highly functional parts and components for cars, which lowers emissions and fuel consumption while enhancing performance and safety. Customers can create and modify their automobiles to suit their preferences thanks to 3D printing's ability to personalize and customize products.

All things considered, 3D printing is expected to keep expanding quickly and become more widely used across a range of industries thanks to developments in software, hardware, and materials. Through the utilization of artificial intelligence, machine learning, and 3D printing, businesses can open up new avenues for innovation, expansion, and a competitive edge in the international market.

Chapter 9: Genomics

New Developments in Healthcare and DNA Analysis

Recent years have seen tremendous advances in genomics, the study of an organism's whole genetic makeup, which have transformed a number of scientific disciplines, including agriculture, healthcare, and agriculture. Understanding genetic illnesses, finding therapeutic targets, and customizing medical therapies have all benefited from the capacity to sequence and analyze complete genomes.

The creation of next-generation sequencing (NGS) technology, which make it possible to quickly and affordably sequence complete genomes, is one of the most noteworthy developments in genomics. Thanks to NGS, researchers can now investigate genetic variants, mutations, and patterns of gene expression throughout the entire genome. This has significantly increased our capacity to analyze DNA.

Precision medicine, a method of treating and diagnosing illnesses that considers individual genetic variations, has been made possible by these developments in DNA sequencing. Doctors can forecast a patient's response to a certain medication, find genetic changes that predispose them to a particular disease, and customize medical interventions by studying the patient's genome.

Because tailored medicines that take advantage of cancer cells' genetic weaknesses have been made possible by genomics, the study and treatment of cancer have undergone a revolutionary change.

Oncologists can prescribe targeted medications that selectively block the growth and spread of cancer cells by identifying actionable mutations through the sequencing of tumor genomes. This can enhance treatment outcomes and increase survival rates for cancer patients.

Genetic Engineering and Bioinformatics Careers

Professionals with expertise in genetics engineering, bioinformatics, and related subjects are in high demand due to the swift expansion of genomics. An essential part in evaluating and deciphering genomic data is the multidisciplinary field of bioinformatics, which blends computer science, biology, and statistics. To help researchers derive valuable insights from large-scale genomics experiments, bioinformaticians provide databases, software tools, and algorithms for storing, analyzing, and visualizing genomic data.

The manipulation and modification of an organism's genetic material for a variety of objectives, including genetic engineering, gene therapy, and synthetic biology, is the specialty of genetics engineers. To precisely alter DNA sequences and investigate the role of genes in living things, genetic engineers employ instruments such as the ground-breaking gene-editing technology CRISPR-Cas9.

Improving Genomic Health and Disease Diagnosis

Because genomics allows for the early identification, precise diagnosis, and focused treatment of genetic illnesses, it has the potential to revolutionize healthcare.

Doctors can detect genetic changes linked to hereditary diseases including Huntington's disease, sickle cell anemia, and cystic fibrosis by examining a person's genome. This enables early intervention and individualized treatment plans.

Genomic analysis is not only being used to diagnose genetic disorders but also to find genetic risk factors for prevalent complicated diseases including cancer, diabetes, and heart disease. Researchers can find novel pharmacological targets and create fresh therapeutic approaches targeted at preventing or treating these illnesses by looking at the genetic foundation of these disorders.

Furthermore, by facilitating the quick and precise identification of pathogens and the tracking of their dissemination throughout human populations, genomics is proving to be a vital tool for infectious disease surveillance and epidemic response. Genomic sequencing has been used, for instance, to follow transmission chains, discover new variations of concern, and monitor the evolution of the SARS-CoV-2 virus during the COVID-19 pandemic.

Let us conclude by saying that genomics is a revolutionary technique that can change scientific research, healthcare, and agriculture. Researchers and medical practitioners can create tailored treatments, learn more about the genetic causes of diseases, and enhance patient outcomes by utilizing the potential of genomics. For those who are interested in making a difference in the field of genomics, there are interesting employment opportunities as the demand for qualified specialists in bioinformatics, genetics engineering, and related subjects only grows as genomics advances.

Chapter 10: New Energy Solutions

Adopting Sustainable Energy Substitutes

The shift to sustainable energy options has become essential as the globe struggles with the pressing need to address climate change and cut greenhouse gas emissions. In order to lessen the effects of climate change and provide a cleaner, greener future for future generations, emerging energy options like solar, wind, hydro, and geothermal power provide renewable and ecologically acceptable alternatives to fossil fuels.

The increasing awareness of renewable energy sources' advantages for the environment and the economy is one of the main forces behind the adoption of new energy solutions. One clean and sustainable energy source is solar energy, which is abundant, endless, and produces no greenhouse emissions when used. Similar to this, wind power uses the wind's kinetic energy to create electricity, providing a clean, renewable fuel substitute for conventional fossil fuels.

Significant potential for innovation, investment, and economic growth are also presented by the switch to new energy alternatives. Global acceptance and deployment of renewable energy technologies, like solar panels, wind turbines, and battery storage systems, have been fueled by their rising cost-competitiveness and scalability. In the field of renewable energy, this has led to the emergence of new markets, businesses, and employment possibilities, promoting economic growth and the shift to a low-carbon economy.

Careers in Climate Strategy, Renewable Technology, and Solar Energy

A growing need for qualified experts in a variety of fields, such as solar energy, climate policy, and renewable technology, has resulted from the move towards new energy solutions. These professions provide the chance to significantly impact climate change mitigation, clean energy technology advancement, and sustainable development.

Solar engineers, technicians, and installers who are capable of designing, constructing, and maintaining solar photovoltaic (PV) systems are needed, for instance, in the solar energy industry. These experts are vital to lowering costs, providing more accessible and reasonably priced solar energy, and hastening the global installation of solar power.

A similar transition to a low-carbon economy and the successful implementation of climate mitigation and adaptation strategies require careers in climate strategy and policy. In order to develop and implement climate policies, legislation, and initiatives that support the deployment of renewable energy, energy efficiency, and the reduction of greenhouse gas emissions, climate strategists, policy analysts, and sustainability consultants collaborate with governments, corporations, and organizations.

Renewable energy sources such as wind, hydropower, biomass, and geothermal energy offer a plethora of job prospects in addition to solar energy and climate strategy. In order to increase the effectiveness, dependability, and affordability of renewable energy generation, storage, and distribution, researchers, engineers, and specialists in renewable technology are working to develop novel technologies, materials, and systems.

Developing Clean Energy to Build a Greener Future

In order to reduce human dependency on fossil fuels and create a more sustainable and greener future, a shift toward new energy solutions is imperative. We can lessen greenhouse gas emissions, slow down climate change, and save the earth for future generations by embracing renewable energy sources like solar, wind, and hydro power.

Adopting new energy solutions also has several advantages outside of protecting the environment, such as increased economic growth, job creation, and energy security. Renewable energy initiatives support the development of resilient and sustainable economies by generating jobs locally, promoting economic growth, and drawing investment to communities worldwide.

In summary, innovative energy solutions provide a revolutionary chance to tackle the pressing issues of sustainable development, energy security, and climate change. We can quicken the shift to a low-carbon economy and create a more successful and environmentally friendly future for all by embracing renewable energy sources, making investments in clean energy technologies, and encouraging innovation and teamwork.

Chapter 11: Robotic Process Automation (RPA)

Software-Assisted Business Process Automation

Robotic Process Automation (RPA) is a disruptive technology that uses software robots, or "bots," to automate repetitive, rule-based processes. In a variety of applications and systems, these bots replicate human activities to carry out tasks like data entry, data extraction, form filling, and report generating. RPA helps businesses to increase accuracy, streamline workflows, and free up human staff to work on more strategic, high-value jobs by automating these repetitive chores.

RPA's ability to interact with current IT systems and applications without the need for intricate coding or system updates is one of its main advantages. RPA bots can employ methods like screen scraping, API integration, and data manipulation to communicate with user interfaces, online applications, databases, and legacy systems. Because of its adaptability, businesses may automate a large number of procedures in a variety of divisions and roles, including human resources, accounting, finance, and customer support.

Rules-based, repetitive, and high-volume processes including data input, invoice processing, payroll processing, and order fulfillment are especially well-suited for robotic process automation (RPA). Organizations may substantially lower errors, enhance compliance, and shorten process cycle times by automating these operations, which will save money and improve operational efficiency.

Job Roles in Solution Architecture and RPA Development

There is a rising need for qualified individuals with experience in RPA development, implementation, and solution architecture due to the increasing use of

RPA across industries. Driving digital transformation projects, working with cutting edge technology, and having a real impact on corporate performance are all possible with a career in robotic process automation (RPA).

An RPA developer's job is one of the most important ones in the field since they design, develop, and maintain RPA bots that automate business processes.

Software development, programming languages, and process automation tools like UiPath, Automation Anywhere, or Blue Prism are common backgrounds for RPA developers. They collaborate closely with stakeholders in the organization to find opportunities for automation, collect requirements, and create bots that satisfy those needs.

An RPA solution architect plays a crucial role in RPA as well. They are in charge of creating end-to-end RPA solutions that solve business problems and produce quantifiable value. In order to design automation strategies, build scalable and resilient bot architectures, and guarantee alignment with company goals and objectives, RPA solution architects collaborate closely with business leaders, IT teams, and RPA developers.

Opportunities exist for RPA business analysts, project managers, and automation consultants in addition to RPA developers and solution architects. These professionals are essential in promoting RPA adoption, overseeing automation initiatives, and optimizing RPA's advantages throughout the company.

Increasing Production and Efficiency with Automation

RPA's capacity to increase productivity and efficiency by automating tedious jobs and processes, lowering manual labor requirements, and shortening process cycle times is one of its main advantages. RPA allows businesses to reallocate human resources to more strategic, value-added jobs that call for creativity, problem-solving, and critical thinking by automating repetitive operations like data input, reconciliation, and report preparation.

Moreover, by removing human error and inconsistent results from manual data entry and processing, RPA can increase process accuracy and compliance. RPA bots decrease the possibility of mistakes, exceptions, and compliance infractions by carrying out activities with accuracy and consistency. This raises consumer satisfaction and trust in addition to improving decision-making and data quality.

Moreover, RPA gives businesses the ability to scale operations more successfully and adapt quickly to changing business needs. Organizations may optimize resources, cut costs, and spur creativity by deploying RPA bots quickly and easily to automate new processes or modify old ones.

In conclusion, by automating repetitive operations, increasing productivity, and promoting digital transformation, robotic process automation, or RPA, is revolutionizing the way businesses run. In today's fast-paced business world, firms can gain a competitive edge, enhance productivity, and streamline processes by utilizing RPA technology and investing in trained individuals.

Chapter 12: Edge Computing

Addressing Latency Issues with Edge Computing

A distributed computing paradigm known as "edge computing" lowers latency and bandwidth consumption by relocating computation and data storage closer to the point of need. Conventional cloud computing relies on centrally located data centers that are remote from end users, which causes processing and transmission of data to be delayed. By bringing computing resources closer to the network's edge, edge computing seeks to address these issues and improve performance for applications that are sensitive to latency. This allows for quicker response times.

Addressing latency issues in real-time applications like Internet of Things (IoT), augmented reality (AR), virtual reality (VR), and autonomous vehicles is one of edge computing's main advantages. Edge computing speeds up decision-making and improves user responsiveness by processing data closer to the source, cutting down on the amount of time it takes for data to move from the device to the cloud and back. Applications that demand low latency, like interactive gaming, industrial automation, and remote monitoring, should pay special attention to this.

Supporting offline or sporadically connected environments, where constant connectivity to the cloud might not be possible, is another benefit of edge computing. With the ability to process and store data locally, edge devices can function independently even in situations where network connectivity is sporadic or unreliable. This makes edge computing viable for mission-critical applications in sectors like manufacturing, transportation, and healthcare, where connectivity failures or downtime can have dire repercussions.

Additionally, by processing sensitive data locally, edge computing lowers the risk of data breaches and unauthorized access while also improving privacy and security. Edge computing assists businesses in adhering to data privacy laws and safeguarding sensitive data from intrusions by reducing the amount of data that must be transmitted over the network. This makes edge computing a desirable choice for sensitive data-handling applications like government, healthcare, and finance.

Cloud Infrastructure and Reliability Engineering Careers

Professionals with experience in reliability engineering and cloud infrastructure now have more opportunities thanks to the growth of edge computing. Edge nodes, gateways, and edge servers are among the infrastructure parts supporting edge computing environments that cloud infrastructure engineers design, implement, and oversee. To guarantee the dependability, scalability, and efficiency of edge computing systems, they collaborate closely with network engineers, software developers, and system administrators.

Contrarily, reliability engineering is concerned with creating and putting into place robust, fault-tolerant systems that are able to endure disruptions such as network outages and hardware failures.

To reduce downtime and guarantee the continuous operation of edge computing infrastructure, reliability engineers employ strategies like load balancing, redundancy, and failover. Additionally, they keep an eye on system performance, examine potential causes of failure, and make adjustments to improve system availability and dependability.

Jobs for edge computing architects, solution architects, and technical consultants who specialize in developing and implementing edge computing solutions for particular use cases and industries are available in addition to those in cloud infrastructure and reliability engineering.

Working closely with clients, these experts evaluate their current infrastructure, ascertain their needs, and create edge computing solutions that are specifically tailored to their requirements.

Data Processing Optimization in Remote Locations

Edge computing is especially useful for applications that need to process and analyze data in real time in dispersed or remote locations where it might not be feasible or feasible to use centralized cloud resources.

In remote or harsh environments, where connectivity may be limited or unreliable, industries like oil and gas, mining, agriculture, and maritime face particular challenges when it comes to gathering, processing, and analyzing data.

Organizations can efficiently process and analyze data in remote locations, extracting actionable insights and facilitating real-time decision-making by deploying edge computing infrastructure closer to the data generation source.

Edge computing, for instance, can be used to optimize production processes in offshore platforms and remote drilling sites, monitor and manage drilling operations, and analyze seismic data in the oil and gas sector.

In a similar vein, edge computing in agriculture can be applied to remote fields and greenhouses to monitor soil conditions, track crop growth, and control irrigation systems. Through local processing of sensor data, edge computing helps farmers maximize resource use, cut back on water usage, and boost crop yields—all of which boost output and profitability.

To sum up, edge computing is a great way to cut down on latency, boost dependability, and maximize data processing in remote areas. Through edge computing, latency-sensitive applications can benefit from real-time insights and improved decision-making by moving computation and data storage closer to the edge of the network.

The field of edge computing is expected to witness significant growth in the need for proficient experts in cloud infrastructure, reliability engineering, and edge computing architecture. This will present promising career prospects for individuals possessing the requisite skills and knowledge.

Chapter 13: Quantum Computing

Data Processing: Using Quantum Phenomena

Utilizing the ideas of quantum physics, quantum computing is a cutting-edge method of computation that enables calculations to be carried out at scales and speeds beyond the capabilities of traditional computers. Quantum computers employ quantum bits, or qubits, which can exist in several states simultaneously due to a phenomena known as superposition. This is in contrast to classical computers, which use bits to represent information as either 0 or 1. As a result, quantum computers can handle enormous volumes of data concurrently and do considerably faster complicated problem solving than traditional computers.

The fact that quantum computing can complete some computations tenfold quicker than traditional computers is one of its main benefits.

For instance, quantum computers are very good at factorsing big numbers, solving optimization issues, and simulating quantum systems—tasks that take too long for classical computers to do. This makes applications in domains like financial modeling, materials science, drug development, and cryptography especially well-suited for quantum computing.

Using entanglement, a phenomena in which qubits become associated with one another so that the state of one depends on the state of another even if they are separated by great distances, is another key component of quantum computing.

Entanglement opens up new possibilities for communication and information processing by enabling quantum computers to execute highly parallelized calculations and transmit information instantaneously over great distances.

Chances in Machine Learning and Quantum Mechanics

For academics and engineers with experience in quantum mechanics, machine learning, and related domains, the emergence of quantum computing has presented fascinating opportunities. Researchers studying quantum mechanics' foundational ideas and creating novel technologies that use quantum phenomena for information processing and computation are led by quantum physicists.

By creating methods and algorithms that take use of the special properties of quantum computers, machine learning specialists are also making significant contributions to the field of quantum computing. Combining methods from both classical and quantum computing, quantum machine learning tackles challenging optimization and pattern recognition tasks and has the potential to transform domains including data analytics, natural language processing, and image recognition.

Furthermore, new paths for innovation and discovery are being opened up by multidisciplinary study at the nexus of quantum computing and other disciplines like chemistry, biology, and finance. Advances in drug discovery, materials design, and renewable energy are being made possible by quantum chemists' use of quantum computers to simulate the behavior of molecules and materials with previously unheard-of accuracy. Comparably, researchers studying quantum computing are examining its potential for simulating intricate biological systems and deciphering the secrets of life at the molecular level.

Computing: Revolutionizing with Quantum Technology

The application of quantum computing has the potential to completely change how we engage with the world around us, solve issues, and process information. Quantum computing promises to have a significant impact on a wide range of fields and sectors, from expediting drug development and reinventing cryptography to enhancing supply chains and logistics.

Quantum computing may make it possible to create new algorithms in the financial sector for fraud detection, risk management, and portfolio optimization. This could result in more reliable and effective financial systems.

By simulating molecular interactions and predicting the efficacy of novel treatments with previously unheard-of accuracy, quantum computing has the potential to transform drug discovery in the healthcare industry and cut the time and expense of bringing new therapeutics to market.

Furthermore, by factoring huge numbers and tackling other challenging computational tasks in polynomial time, quantum computing has the potential to make current encryption systems obsolete in the field of cybersecurity. In order to secure sensitive data in a post-quantum future, academics have been motivated to create new cryptographic protocols and encryption algorithms that are immune to quantum attacks.

To sum up, quantum computing is a paradigm change in computing technology that has significant ramifications for business, academia, and society at large. Quantum computing has the ability to address some of the most important issues confronting humanity and open up new avenues for creativity and discovery by utilizing the power of quantum physics to carry out computations that are beyond the capabilities of conventional computers. The need for qualified experts in quantum mechanics, machine learning, and related topics is predicted to increase as quantum computing develops, offering individuals with the necessary training and experience fascinating job options.

Chapter 14: Augmented and Virtual Reality

Enhancing Experiences in Gaming, Training, and Marketing

Two cutting-edge technologies that have the power to completely change how we interact with digital material and the real world are virtual reality (VR) and augmented reality (AR). While AR superimposes digital data on the physical world, VR immerses users in a fully virtual experience. Thanks to developments in content creation tools, hardware, and software, these technologies have advanced quickly in recent years.

VR and AR gaming technologies provide immersive experiences that meld the virtual and real worlds together. Through the use of specialized gear, such as VR headgear and motion controllers, gamers can enter fully realized virtual environments while engaging in VR gaming.

This produces a level of immersion and presence that is unmatched by traditional gaming experiences. Contrarily, augmented reality gaming superimposes digital features over the real world, enabling users to interact with virtual characters and objects in their actual surroundings. This makes location-based experiences, social gaming, and interactive narrative all more possible.

Beyond only entertainment, virtual reality and augmented reality are transforming education and training through immersive and dynamic learning environments. VR training simulations, which range from flight simulation and job training to medical procedures and emergency response training, let users hone skills and scenarios in a secure and regulated setting.

AR educational apps improve on traditional learning materials by superimposing digital annotations, descriptions, and interactive features on real-world items and surroundings. This increases learning efficiency and engagement.

VR and AR provide creative opportunities for marketers and advertisers to interact with consumers and build memorable brand experiences. Through virtual reality (VR) marketing initiatives, businesses can take customers to virtual spaces where they can interact with merchandise, browse virtual storefronts, and take part in immersive brand experiences.

Through the use of mobile devices' cameras and sensors, augmented reality (AR) advertising campaigns allow users to interact with virtual goods and experiences in their own surroundings.

Professions in Software Development, Creative Direction, and Game Design

There is a growing need for qualified specialists in a variety of fields, such as software development, game design, and creative direction, due to the rapid expansion of VR and AR technology.

Through the creation of virtual worlds, characters, and gameplay mechanics that take advantage of the special features offered by VR and AR platforms, game designers play a critical role in producing immersive and compelling experiences. In addition to developing code, improving performance, and integrating hardware and software components to create seamless experiences, software developers also specialize in creating the underlying technology and infrastructure that supports VR and AR apps. As they lead groups of artists, designers, and developers to create immersive experiences, creative directors are in charge of the overall creative vision and direction of VR and AR projects.

Artists, animators, sound designers, and writers can contribute their skills to immersive storytelling experiences through VR and AR, in addition to typical game development responsibilities. The 3D models, textures, and animations made by artists and animators give virtual landscapes and characters life, and the immersive audio experiences created by sound designers heighten the sensation of presence and immersion. Writers create unique experiences that strike a chord with audiences by crafting gripping storylines and dialogue that captivate players and advance the plot.

Building the Immersion Technologies of the Future

The way we work, play, and engage with the world around us is about to change as virtual reality and augmented reality technologies develop and grow. VR and AR present a plethora of creative and inventive opportunities, ranging from captivating gaming experiences and interactive training simulations to creative marketing campaigns and educational uses. VR and AR experiences will likely become more and more ingrained in our daily lives, changing the ways in which we interact, study, shop, and communicate as the technology gets more widely available and more reasonably priced.

Finally, it should be noted that VR and AR represent a paradigm change in computing technology with significant ramifications for a variety of sectors and uses.

VR and AR have the power to completely change the way we interact with digital information and the world around us by offering immersive, interactive experiences that appeal to the senses and make it difficult to distinguish between the real and virtual worlds. Exciting employment opportunities for people with the necessary abilities and expertise will arise as VR and AR development becomes more and more in-demand as technology continues to evolve and mature.

Chapter 15: Blockchain

Beyond Cryptocurrencies: Securing Data Transactions

Although it was first used to power cryptocurrencies like Bitcoin, blockchain technology has now developed into a force that is transforming a number of different industries. Fundamentally, blockchain is a distributed, decentralized ledger system that safely logs transactions via an internet of computers. Because blockchain offers immutability, security, and transparency in contrast to traditional centralized databases, it is perfect for a variety of uses outside of finance.

The capacity of blockchain to safeguard data transactions using cryptographic methods is one of its primary characteristics. Every transaction is documented in a "block" and connected chronologically in a "chain," resulting in an impenetrable record of every transaction. By guaranteeing that data cannot be changed or removed without the agreement of all network users, this promotes a high degree of integrity and confidence.

Blockchain technology has the ability to completely transform data interactions in a number of different sectors, including government, real estate, healthcare, and supply chain management. Blockchain technology can be used in supply chain management to give products end-to-end visibility and traceability, enabling businesses to monitor the flow of goods from the manufacturer to the customer.

Blockchain in healthcare can be used to safely store and exchange medical data, protecting patient privacy and facilitating interoperability between various healthcare providers.

Blockchain technology has the potential to improve transparency in the purchasing and selling of real estate by streamlining transactions and lowering fraud. Blockchain technology has the potential to improve government accountability and transparency in areas like voting, identity management, and taxation.

Career Opportunities in Cryptography and Risk Analysis

The increasing use of blockchain technology has increased demand for qualified individuals with knowledge of cryptography and risk assessment.

Risk analysts are essential in identifying and reducing the possible risks connected to blockchain deployments, including operational difficulties, security flaws, and compliance issues. Risk analysts assist companies in navigating the challenges of adopting blockchain technology and guaranteeing the security and integrity of their data transactions by carrying out thorough risk assessments and creating risk management plans.

Blockchain technology is based on cryptography, the science of protecting data and communications against unwanted access. To encrypt and decrypt data, authenticate users, and guarantee the confidentiality, integrity, and validity of data transactions on the blockchain, cryptographers create and put into practice cryptographic algorithms and protocols. Cryptographers are essential in protecting sensitive data and reducing cyber risks because to the growing significance of cybersecurity and data privacy.

Blockchain Technology Transforming Industries

Blockchain technology has the power to revolutionize entire sectors by offering cutting-edge fixes for enduring problems and inefficiencies. Blockchain reduces the need for middlemen and streamlines financial sector operations including stocks trading, remittances, and cross-border payments by enabling faster, more secure, and more affordable transactions. Blockchain enhances accountability, traceability, and transparency in supply chain management, allowing businesses to track the origin and authenticity of products and lower the danger of counterfeit goods.

Blockchain improves patient privacy, interoperability, and data security in the healthcare industry. This makes it easier to interchange medical records and provides tailored healthcare solutions.

Blockchain facilitates property transactions in real estate by removing the need for middlemen and lowering the possibility of fraud, assuring openness and confidence in the purchasing and selling procedure.

Blockchain improves accountability, efficiency, and transparency in government services by facilitating digital identity management, safe and impenetrable voting systems, and open funding distribution.

To sum up, blockchain technology has the potential to completely transform data transactions in a variety of industries by offering transparent, safe, and effective answers to enduring problems and inefficiencies.

Blockchain provides unmatched security, immutability, and transparency through its distributed and decentralized ledger technology, which makes it perfect for a variety of uses outside of cryptocurrency. The demand for qualified experts in risk analysis, cryptography, and blockchain development is predicted to rise as businesses continue to investigate the possibilities of blockchain technology. For individuals with the necessary training and experience, this will open up intriguing new career paths.

Chapter 16: Internet of Things (IoT)

Linking Devices to Share Data

The network of networked objects that are equipped with sensors, software, and other technologies that allow them to gather and share data via the internet is known as the Internet of Things (IoT). These gadgets might be anything from commonplace items like wearables, cellphones, and household appliances to machinery used in industry, transportation, and infrastructure. IoT makes it possible for these gadgets to share and communicate data seamlessly, which improves efficiency, automation, and convenience in a variety of personal and professional contexts.

The idea of connectedness, which enables real-time communication between objects and users, is at the core of the Internet of Things.

Numerous wireless communication technologies, such as Wi-Fi, Bluetooth, Zigbee, and cellular networks, enable this connectivity. IoT devices can remotely monitor, operate, and automate a variety of systems and processes by using these technologies to transfer data to centralized servers or other connected devices.

The capacity of IoT to produce enormous amounts of data from sensors and devices—often referred to as "big data"—is one of its main advantages. Organizations can utilize this data to make data-driven choices, optimize operations, and enhance customer experiences by learning vital insights about asset performance, environmental conditions, user behavior, and other critical metrics.

IoT is transforming how we connect with the world around us and opening up new possibilities for innovation and growth, from smart homes and cities to industrial automation and healthcare.

Professions in Hardware Interfacing and Information Security

The demand for experts in hardware interface and information security is rising as IoT continues to spread throughout various businesses and sectors. When it comes to guaranteeing the availability, confidentiality, and integrity of data conveyed by Internet of Things devices and systems, information security specialists are essential. They create and put into practice access rules, encryption methods, and security protocols to guard against theft, unauthorized access, and modification of sensitive data.

On the other side, experts in hardware interfacing concentrate on the creation, design, and integration of hardware parts and sensors utilized in Internet of Things devices.

To guarantee smooth connectivity and device compatibility, they collaborate closely with engineers, designers, and manufacturers to choose and configure the proper hardware parts, interface protocols, and communication standards. Hardware interfacing experts optimize hardware functionality and performance to allow Internet of Things devices to gather precise data and communicate efficiently over the internet.

Using IoT Technology to Build a Connected World

IoT technology is transforming how we live and work by establishing a networked ecosystem of tools, services, and systems that improve quality of life, productivity, and efficiency. Comfort, safety, and energy efficiency are all increased in smart homes thanks to the remote management and monitoring capabilities of Internet of Things (IoT) devices like voice assistants, security cameras, and thermostats. Smart city planners may optimize urban infrastructure and services for sustainability and resilience by using data collected from IoT sensors and networks on traffic flow, air quality, and waste management.

IoT-enabled machinery and devices in industrial settings optimize manufacturing processes, track equipment performance, and anticipate maintenance requirements, lowering downtime and raising productivity.

IoT technologies in the healthcare industry, such as smart medical devices, wearable fitness trackers, and remote patient monitoring systems, allow healthcare practitioners to provide individualized, data-driven care while also empowering patients to take charge of their health and well-being. IoT technology is transforming every area of our lives and opening up new possibilities for innovation and growth, from retail and entertainment to transportation and agriculture.

To sum up, the Internet of Things, or IoT, is a revolutionary technology that is changing the way people engage with the environment. IoT facilitates smooth data interchange, communication, and automation by linking systems and devices to the internet. This increases productivity, convenience, and efficiency in a variety of spheres of life and business. The demand for experts in information security, hardware interface, and other specialized fields is rising as IoT develops and grows because they can spur innovation and help to influence the direction of linked technology.

Chapter 17: 5G

Transforming Communication at Quicker Speeds

The fifth generation (5G) of wireless technology is expected to transform connection by providing higher capacities, lower latency, and quicker speeds than previous generations. 5G, which has speeds up to 100 times faster than 4G LTE, is perfect for a variety of applications, including augmented reality and mobile gaming, autonomous vehicles, and smart cities. It also allows for ultra-fast downloads, seamless streaming, and real-time communication.

The utilization of millimeter waves, or higher frequency bands, which allow for quicker data transfer over shorter distances, is one of 5G's primary advances. 5G networks may support multiple gigabit speeds and a large number of connected devices concurrently by utilizing these higher frequencies. This allows for the connection of everything from smartphones and tablets to Internet of Things sensors and self-driving drones.

5G promises much reduced latency, or delay, in addition to speed, which is essential for applications like remote surgery, driverless cars, and industrial automation that need real-time communication and response. 5G offers instantaneous engagement and feedback with latency as low as one millisecond, creating new opportunities for innovation and disruption across a range of industries.

Telecom and App Development Opportunities

Telecom corporations, gadget makers, and app developers have a lot of options to profit from the revolutionary potential of 5G technology as it rolls out. In order to accommodate 5G infrastructure, telecom companies are spending billions of dollars modernizing their networks. This includes installing new base stations, antennas, and fiber optic cables to increase capacity and coverage.

In response to the increasing consumer demand for faster speeds and greater connectivity, device manufacturers are working feverishly to create and ship smartphones, tablets, and other connected devices that are compatible with 5G.

App developers now have the chance to produce cutting-edge services and applications that take advantage of 5G networks' speed, latency, and capacity to offer immersive experiences and unleash new capabilities as 5G-enabled devices become more and more commonplace.

5G gives up a world of possibilities for developers to create transformative experiences that were previously not conceivable with 4G LTE, from telemedicine and cloud gaming to augmented reality and virtual reality. Developers can transform the way we work, play, and communicate by utilizing 5G to power apps that facilitate smooth streaming, real-time collaboration, and immersive multimedia consumption.

Building the Future of Connectivity and Communication

By facilitating a new era of digital innovation and disruption, 5G is positioned to influence the direction of connection and communication in the future. With its extremely low latency, enormous capacity, and lightning-fast speeds, 5G promises to change entire industries, boost productivity, and improve living conditions for billions of people worldwide.

5G in the healthcare industry makes robotic surgery, telemedicine, and remote patient monitoring possible. These innovations improve access to healthcare services, save costs, and enable healthcare practitioners to provide better care and outcomes.

5G is enabling connected infrastructure, intelligent traffic management systems, and driverless cars in the transportation sector, opening the door to more sustainable, safe, and effective mobility options.

5G in manufacturing makes it possible to monitor and control industrial processes in real time, do predictive maintenance, and use autonomous robots, all of which increase productivity, efficiency, and flexibility in factory operations. 5G will change the way we consume and interact with media and entertainment by enabling immersive experiences, interactive gaming, and live streaming of high-definition material.

In summary, 5G is a revolutionary technology that will completely change the way we live, work, and communicate in the digital age. It is not just a quicker version of 4G LTE. 5G offers up a world of opportunities for innovation and disruption across industries, from healthcare and transportation to manufacturing and entertainment, with its unparalleled speed, low latency, and vast capacity. 5G will influence communication and connectivity in the future as it spreads over the world, propelling future technological advancements, social advancements, and economic prosperity.

Chapter 18: Cybersecurity

Evolving Threats and Defense Mechanisms

In the linked world of today, cybersecurity has emerged as a major issue for all parties—individuals, companies, and governments. Cybercriminals' methods and strategies for taking advantage of weaknesses and compromising private data are evolving along with technology. The threat landscape is always changing, presenting new difficulties for cybersecurity professionals tasked with protecting against these threats. These dangers range from ransomware and phishing assaults to data breaches and identity theft.

The vastness and intricacy of contemporary IT ecosystems are one of the main obstacles to cybersecurity. Organizations now have a plethora of possible attack vectors that can be leveraged by cybercriminals due to the widespread use of digital platforms, cloud services, and linked devices.

A more proactive and comprehensive strategy to cybersecurity is needed since traditional security measures, including firewalls and antivirus software, are no longer adequate to defend against sophisticated cyber threats.

Professionals in cybersecurity utilize various protection mechanisms and best practices to safeguard against cyber threats in order to tackle these difficulties.

This entails putting strong authentication and access controls in place, encrypting sensitive data both in transit and at rest, and routinely patching and updating software to fix known vulnerabilities.

In order to find and fix possible security flaws before bad actors can take advantage of them, businesses also frequently do regular security assessments and penetration tests.

Security engineering and ethical hacking careers

Career prospects in the dynamic and rapidly expanding sector of cybersecurity are developing in tandem with the need for cybersecurity specialists. As a penetration tester or white-hat hacker, ethical hacking is one of the most sought-after careers in cybersecurity. It is the duty of ethical hackers to find and take advantage of security flaws in order to evaluate how well an organization's security defenses work and to assist reduce any dangers.

Apart from ethical hacking, cybersecurity offers other job options such as security engineering, incident response, threat intelligence analysis, and security architecture. These positions call for a wide range of abilities, including risk management, network security, cryptography, and safe coding techniques.

Strong analytical abilities, meticulousness, and in-depth knowledge of the most recent cyberthreats and attack strategies are prerequisites for success in the field of cybersecurity.

Along with upholding moral principles and professional codes of behavior, they also need to stay current on new developments in cybersecurity trends and technology.

Securing Privacy and Digital Safety in a Linked World

There has never been a more crucial time to protect the privacy and security of digital assets and information in our increasingly digital and linked world. Organizations need to be proactive in guarding against cyber risks and preventing unauthorized access to or disclosure of sensitive information, including financial and personal data, intellectual property, and vital infrastructure.

In order to do this, businesses need to take a multi-layered strategy to cybersecurity that blends administrative and technical controls, including security policies, procedures, and training initiatives, with intrusion detection systems, firewalls, and encryption. In order to handle new threats and vulnerabilities, they must also continuously evaluate and upgrade their security posture.

Finally, they must promote a culture of security awareness and accountability among workers, contractors, and outside vendors.

To sum up, cybersecurity is an essential part of our digital society since it safeguards private and digital assets while defending people, organizations, and governments from online attacks. People may play a critical part in protecting our digital future and creating a more secure and resilient cyber landscape for future generations by choosing a profession in cybersecurity and keeping up with developing threats and defense methods.

Chapter 19: Full Stack Development

Using Full Stack Development to Develop End-to-End Solutions

Web applications that incorporate both the front-end (client-side) and back-end (server-side) components are referred to as full stack development. The broad range of technologies and programming languages that full stack developers are skilled in enables them to create end-to-end solutions that satisfy the requirements of contemporary online applications.

Full stack development's adaptability and flexibility are two of its main benefits. From creating server-side logic and managing databases to designing user interfaces and implementing front-end functionality, full stack engineers are equipped with the knowledge and abilities to work on every part of the development process. This enables them to approach development holistically and produce unified, integrated solutions that benefit end users.

Full stack engineers have a great grasp of software architecture and design principles in addition to their technical expertise. They are also highly adept at addressing problems. They can effectively handle intricate development tasks and make well-informed choices on scalability, performance optimization, and technology choice.

Using Versatile Skills to Streamline Development Processes

Agile and iterative development approaches that prioritize fast iteration, adaptability, and teamwork, like Scrum and Kanban, are ideal for full stack development.

Full stack developers can work more productively and successfully in agile teams, contributing to all phases of the development lifecycle, thanks to their broad skill set that encompasses both front-end and back-end technologies.

In addition, full stack developers know how to automate tedious work and speed up the development process by utilizing a range of frameworks and development tools.

This covers libraries and frameworks for front-end and back-end development, as well as tools for build automation, testing, deployment, and version control.

Full stack developers are able to produce high-quality software solutions that satisfy changing user and stakeholder needs while also speeding up the development process and decreasing time-to-market by utilizing their diverse skill set.

Building Innovative Software Solutions with Full Stack Developer

Organizations are under increasing pressure to innovate and set themselves apart through technology in today's fast-paced and competitive business climate. In this process, full stack developers are essential to an organization's success since they assist in creating creative software solutions that promote growth.

The capacity of full stack development to combine various systems and technologies to produce smooth and coherent user experiences is one of its main advantages. Full stack developers are able to create and execute solutions that bridge the gap between user interfaces and underlying business logic by utilizing their expertise in front-end and back-end technologies.

Furthermore, full stack developers frequently participate in every stage of the creation of a product, from conception and prototyping to execution and launch. As a result, they are able to provide insightful opinions and creative ideas throughout the development process, as well as a thorough understanding of the product's requirements and vision.

In conclusion, the ability to create end-to-end solutions that satisfy the requirements of contemporary online applications is made possible by the varied and in-demand skill set of full stack development. Full stack developers are able to provide creative software solutions that promote business growth and success by utilizing their diverse skill set and experience to expedite time-to-market and streamline development procedures.

Chapter 20: DevOps

Cooperation between the Teams of Operations and Development

A combination of the words "development" and "operations," DevOps is a set of procedures and cultural values meant to enhance communication between teams working on software development and IT operations. In the past, these two teams operated independently, with operations teams handling infrastructure and deployment and developers concentrating on producing code. But this strategy frequently resulted in inefficiencies, snags, and disputes amongst groups.

DevOps aims to remove these obstacles and promote a shared accountability, communication, and teamwork culture. DevOps seeks to optimize the software development lifecycle, from code commit to deployment, by combining the development and operations teams. This ensures that software is provided promptly, dependably, and effectively.

Automation is one of the core ideas of DevOps. Teams may minimize errors, speed up software update delivery, and decrease manual labor by automating repetitive operations like code builds, testing, and deployment. This enables businesses to provide value to clients more quickly and adapt more swiftly to the shifting demands of the market.

Additionally, DevOps promotes a shift-left in software development, integrating quality assurance and testing earlier in the process. This lowers the chance of errors and guarantees that software satisfies quality requirements before to being put into production by assisting in the earlier identification and resolution of problems.

Using DevOps Practices to Improve Software Quality and Deployment

Software quality and deployment procedures can be enhanced by using a variety of techniques and tools that are included in the DevOps suite. Continuous integration (CI) is one such technique in which developers periodically integrate their code modifications into a shared repository, starting automated build and testing procedures. This lowers the possibility of integration problems later on by enabling teams to find and address integration mistakes early in the development cycle.

Continuous delivery (CD), which continuously deploys code changes to environments similar to production for testing and validation, is another essential technique. Teams may now quickly and often upgrade software without compromising on stability or quality thanks to this.

Moreover, DevOps promotes the automation of infrastructure resource supply and management through the usage of infrastructure as code, or IaC.

Teams may increase consistency, lower the chance of configuration drift, and quickly spin up and shut down environments by describing infrastructure configurations in code.

In general, DevOps approaches assist companies in lowering time-to-market, increasing deployment frequency, and improving software quality, all of which help them react faster to demands from customers and rivals.

Guiding Software Development and Deployment Towards Its Future

The future of software development and deployment is probably going to be more automated, collaborative, and agile as long as companies keep implementing DevOps principles. In addition to being a collection of procedures and technologies, DevOps is a cultural movement that calls on businesses to welcome change, adjust to new methods of operation, and always strive for improvement.

Beyond simply development and operations teams, we should anticipate seeing more firms adopt DevOps ideas in the future. To better provide value to customers, this may entail tighter coordination with other business divisions like marketing, sales, and customer service.

Furthermore, the adoption of DevOps approaches is probably going to pick up speed due to the emergence of cloud computing, microservices designs, and containerization technologies. The adaptability, scalability, and agility required to enable contemporary software development and deployment processes are offered by these technologies.

To sum up, DevOps is changing how businesses create and implement software, allowing them to provide value to clients more quickly and effectively. DevOps methods assist firms stay ahead in a market that is becoming more and more competitive by promoting collaboration, automation, and continuous improvement. These practices also help organizations manage the difficulties of modern software development and deployment.

Chapter 21: Metaverse

Building Digital Environments That Are Virtually Interconnected

When physical reality, augmented reality (AR), virtual reality (VR), and other immersive technologies come together, a collective virtual shared space known as the metaverse is created. The boundaries between the real and virtual worlds are blurred when users engage in real-time interactions with one another and digital environments in the metaverse.

The interconnectedness of the metaverse is one of its distinguishing characteristics. In contrast to conventional virtual worlds that are frequently fragmented and unconnected, the metaverse is intended to be a smooth and integrated digital landscape.

This implies that users can navigate between various virtual environments, engage with other users and digital objects, and take part in platform- and device-wide shared experiences.

A number of technologies, such as motion tracking devices, haptic feedback systems, virtual reality headsets, and spatial computing platforms, are necessary to create the metaverse. With the aid of these technologies, users can engage with digital objects and immerse themselves in virtual environments by making natural gestures and movements.

Impact on Business Collaboration, Entertainment, and Communication

The metaverse has the power to fundamentally transform business collaboration, entertainment, and communication. The metaverse presents novel avenues for social interaction and connection in terms of communication. In virtual spaces, users can congregate to communicate, work together on projects, attend conferences and events virtually, and even take part in virtual rites and ceremonies.

The metaverse creates new opportunities for interactive experiences, gaming, and immersive storytelling in the entertainment industry. Players can completely submerge themselves in virtual reality games and experiences, exploring fanciful landscapes, working puzzles, and interacting in real-time with other players. Artists can reach a global audience and create unique multimedia experiences that go beyond the confines of physical venues with the help of virtual concerts, performances, and events.

In terms of business, the metaverse presents fresh chances for cooperation, creativity, and efficiency. Regardless of their physical location, remote teams can collaborate in real-time with virtual offices and meeting spaces. While virtual trade shows, exhibitions, and product launches allow businesses to present their offerings to a worldwide audience, immersive training and simulation environments give staff members access to real-world training opportunities in a secure environment.

Investigating Immersive Technologies' Prospects in the Metaverse

The potential for the metaverse is almost endless as immersive technologies advance and develop further. We may anticipate seeing even more sophisticated motion tracking tools, haptic feedback systems, and virtual reality headsets in the future that provide a more realistic and immersive experience.

Furthermore, more sophisticated and responsive virtual environments will be possible thanks to developments in artificial intelligence, machine learning, and natural language processing. Users will receive individualized help and support from chatbots and virtual assistants, and virtual avatars will get more expressive and lifelike.

The metaverse will lead to the emergence of new mediums for digital storytelling, entertainment, and art. In order to create immersive worlds and experiences that enthrall and inspire audiences, virtual reality filmmakers, game developers, and immersive experience designers will push the envelope of creativity and innovation.

All things considered, the metaverse marks a daring new chapter in communication, creativity, and human-computer interaction. The metaverse holds the potential to fundamentally and unexpectedly alter our way of living, working, and playing by merging the most recent technological advancements with our intrinsic need for expression and connection. The metaverse will develop and grow as we investigate and test immersive technologies further, providing fresh chances for inquiry, learning, and cooperation in the digital era.

Chapter 22: Digital Twins

Digital Copies of Real-World Items and Operations

Digital twins are computer-generated images of real-world systems, processes, or things. The data from sensors, Internet of Things (IoT) devices, and other sources are used to construct these digital representations, which are then used to replicate and study the performance and behavior of the corresponding real-world entities.

Digital twins were first introduced in the manufacturing industry, where they were used to simulate and optimize production lines and machinery through virtual models. Since then, though, digital twins have been used in a wider range of industries, such as healthcare, urban planning, transportation, and more.

The sophistication of digital twins varies; they can be as simple as representations of individual objects or components or as complex as simulations of complete environments or systems. Digital twins give organizations the ability to track, evaluate, and improve the performance of their operations and assets in a virtual setting, regardless of how complicated they are.

Digital Twins: Optimising Decision Making and Efficiency

Enhancing productivity and decision-making in a variety of businesses is one of the main advantages of digital twins. Organizations can get real-time insights into their behavior and performance by building virtual representations of physical things and processes. This enables them to see inefficiencies, foresee issues, and make data-driven decisions.

Digital twins, for instance, can be used to mimic production processes in the manufacturing industry and spot bottlenecks or potential areas for improvement. Organizations may monitor key performance indicators (KPIs) including equipment usage, energy consumption, and product quality by analyzing data from sensors and Internet of Things (IoT) devices implanted in production equipment. They can then use this information to manage their operations in real-time.

Digital twins can also be utilized in the healthcare industry to build virtual representations of patients and medical equipment for individualized treatment planning and monitoring. Healthcare professionals can monitor patients' vital signs, medication compliance, and illness progression by analyzing data from wearable sensors and medical devices. They can then utilize this information to customize treatment plans and treatments for each patient.

Digital Twin Technology: Shaping the Future of Simulation and Analysis

The possible uses for digital twin technology are growing into more and more fascinating fields as it develops and grows. Digital twins are being employed in a variety of industries, including manufacturing, healthcare, energy, and urban planning.

Digital twins, for instance, can be used in urban planning to build virtual representations of infrastructure and cities so that the effects of environmental changes, transportation schemes, and urban development projects can be simulated and studied. Urban planners can simulate traffic patterns, energy consumption, air quality, and other characteristics by evaluating data from sensors, satellite imaging, and other sources. They can then use this information to influence policy creation and decision-making.

Similar to this, digital twins can be used in the transportation industry to build virtual representations of cars, highways, and traffic patterns in order to simulate and improve transportation networks. Transportation planners can predict traffic patterns, optimize routes, and raise the effectiveness and safety of transportation networks by evaluating data from traffic cameras, car sensors, and other sources.

All things considered, digital twin technology has the power to completely change how we create, observe, and oversee tangible things and procedures. Organizations can improve their performance, acquire important insights into their operations, and make better decisions by building virtual versions of the real world. This can ultimately result in increased productivity, sustainability, and efficiency across a variety of industries and areas.

Conclusion

Grasping the Chances Provided by the Tech Horizon

It is evident that we are at the dawn of a new era as we come to the close of our investigation of the various technology trends that are reshaping our environment. Technology is advancing at a breakneck pace, taking us into new frontiers where the lines separating the virtual and real worlds are getting fuzzier. We must grasp the chance to mold the future of our world and accept the prospects brought forth by the technological horizon in this constantly shifting landscape.

Emerging technologies like extended reality, quantum computing, and generative AI have the potential to change many industries and open up new avenues for opportunity. These technologies are changing the way we work, live, and interact with the world around us.

They are also improving gaming and entertainment experiences and redefining content creation. We can use technology to stimulate creativity, promote innovation, and address some of the most important problems confronting humanity if we take advantage of these opportunities.

Charting the Course for Careers in Technology

The future of technology careers is growing more dynamic and diverse as the field continues to expand at an unparalleled rate. While whole new professional positions are emerging in sectors like data science, cybersecurity, and artificial intelligence, traditional roles in domains like software development and IT management are expanding to embrace new skills and competences.

To be competitive and relevant in the job market, professionals must change and adapt their skill sets in this quickly changing terrain. To stay up to date with the most recent advancements in technology, this may call for constant learning, upskilling, and reskilling. By remaining adaptable and proactive in our professional growth, we can set ourselves up for success in the digital economy and take advantage of the numerous opportunities that developing technologies bring.

Emerging Technologies: Shaping a Better Future

It is evident as we look to the future that new technology have the power to create a more affluent and happy society for everyone. Technology possesses the ability to instigate constructive social transformation and enhance the well-being of individuals worldwide, ranging from transforming healthcare and education to tackling issues like inequality and climate change.

It is our duty to make sure that these technologies are created and used in an ethical and responsible manner, as tremendous power comes with great responsibility. In order to prevent hazards and abuses, it is necessary to carefully evaluate the ethical implications of developing technologies and to implement strong regulatory frameworks.

We can create a future that is equitable, sustainable, and inclusive for all by cooperating to fully utilize the potential of emerging technology. We can create a better future for future generations by valuing invention, encouraging teamwork, and putting the common good first.

To sum up, there are countless chances for innovation, development, and advancement in the tech world. We can fully utilize technology to create a better society if we seize the opportunities offered by developing technologies, navigate the ever changing field of technology careers, and work for a brighter future for all. Together, with hope, tenacity, and a common goal for a better tomorrow, let's set off on this trip.

www.ingramcontent.com/pod-product-compliance
Lightning Source LLC
Chambersburg PA
CBHW071244050326
40690CB00011B/2252